M. McGregor

A New System of Horse Training or Horse Educating

M. McGregor

A New System of Horse Training or Horse Educating

ISBN/EAN: 9783337046934

Printed in Europe, USA, Canada, Australia, Japan

Cover: Foto ©Lupo / pixelio.de

More available books at **www.hansebooks.com**

A NEW SYSTEM

OF

HORSE-TRAINING,

OR HORSE

EDUCATING,

AS TAUGHT BY

PROFESSOR M. McGREGOR,

ONEIDA, NEW YORK.

TRENTON, ONT.
PRINTED AT THE "COURIER" BOOK AND JOB OFFICE.

PREFACE.

The subject of horsemanship is so closely allied and identified with all man's interests, that everything that can be said to promote a reform in that particular cannot but commend itself to every one interested in that noble animal, and who is there that is not? For amongst the great number of animals under the control of man, the horse is the most serviceable—the most common transactions of every day life cannot tbe consummated without his aid. This book is not presented to the public as an unexceptionable treatise on the horse. It is merely a plain practical exposition of the best system of horsemanship. In order to gratify a desire expressed by those who have witnessed my operations, I write this book—which size is calculated for the pocket—explanatory of the system, so that many things that otherwise might escape their notice, can at any moment be refreshed by a reference to the book. I will try to make every move with the horse so plain, and intelligible, that those who have never witnessed my operations can take hold of and manage the wildest colt, or the most vicious horse. While I beg, from the scrutinizing public, a charitable criticism for any short-comings that may be discovered, I yet feel great confidence that the work will meet with a hearty approval from hosemen generally, as it is my object to be useful rather than offend or appear learned. It is also my wish that this work will prove a valuable auxiliary in bringing about that much needed reform in the proper management and control of the most noble of the brute creation.

THE AUTHOR.

PROF. M. McGREGOR'S

NEW SYSTEM OF

HORSE-TRAINING.

NATURE of the HORSE.

Differing from most men ; I claim that horses have reasoning faculties, at least, to the limit of their experience. They reason from effect to cause ; hence we can only teach them by acts alone. Literally, with the horse, "acts speak louder than words," and hence the absolute importance of commencing every movement with the horse right. No animal has memory equal to that of a horse, and none will reciprocate a kindness or resent an injury sooner.

He is a close observer of everything passing about him. We cannot move or take any particular attitude or hardly give an unusual expression of the face or voice, without its being observed and having some meaning with the horse. Hence we should never show fear, anger, or excitement, but always be cool and determined. There are no two horses whose habits and disposition arc precisely alike, and we should always try to ascertain as much of the character of the horse as possible, before we begin to handle him, so that every movement we make may have some desired effect on the horse's mind. Yet, notwithstanding, there are no two horses whose dispositions are alike, there are certain things that effect all horses alike, namely :

First, ENCOURAGEMENT. When you pat and caress the horse, you say to him that whatever he is doing is right. You have only to get the horse to kick at you, balk, or draw, and then caress him for it and he will do it again, when you ask him ; for he thinks it is right. So never touch the horse until he has done what you ask, and then never fail to caress and encourage.

Second, How HE LEARNS. You cannot teach the horse a word of the English language without a sign ; that is, you must either show him or force the body to move, for a forced move of the horse's body is a sign to him, and is equivalent, in his mind, to a willing move, if you only assure him by caressing afterwards that he has done what you want. So never ask the horse to do any thing, without you are in a position to force obedience.

If you wish to teach the horse a word of command, repeat the word just before you give the sign; and he will soon learn to make the move without the sign.

Third, How THEY JUDGE OF OBJECTS OF FEAR. All horses judge of the objects of fear by the touch of the muscle of the upper lip, or by the smell. It is not so much the looks of an object that frightens the horse as the thought of personal injury. His nose is his fingers, and when he can once feel of an object and satisfy himself that it will not hurt him, he will not care for its appearance. So do not strike with the whip ; for he will think it is the object that hurts him, and will always shy from it. Thoroughly control his mouth, so that he neither dare turn to the right or left, run back or go ahead, when he hears " whoa," then give him time to examine it.

Fourth, WHERE TO CONTROL THE HORSE. Much of my theory depends upon the important fact, that when you control the horse's mouth, you control his whole body. I care not what the habit is, if I can work at the mouth at the time, I will break it up ; yet there are certain habits, as jumping fences, &c., where it is not convenient to get at the mouth at the time, and other means must be resorted to. The horse may drive on ever so light a rein, ordinarily, but do not be deceived, whenever he attempts to kick, run, shy, or bolt, you have no control of his mouth. You have only to control the horse's mouth so that you can rid him of the fear of his heels, and he will cease kicking. Make him relax the muscles of the mouth and give in to a side rein, and he will cease bolting or shying. Keep his attention on the bit and he will cease looking for objects to shy at.

Fifth, SIGNS OF A HORSE HAVING YIELDED. When the horse yields submissively, he will relax the muscles of every part of his body. When the horse sets the muscles of the limbs rigid and stiff, you cannot handle them without being in danger of getting kicked ; for that is the way he tells you, that he is not willing you should touch him. Some people have supposed, that if the horse had a stiff dock it was a sign that he was a strong horse, but I consider it a sure sign, that he is afraid of his tail, and inclined to kick ; for you have only to rid him of the fear, and he will relax the muscles and give up the tail. The horse generally shows fear and anger, by setting the muscles of the ears, inclining them back, distending the muscles of the eyes and nostrels, and hugging the tail. · You must know that the horse has relaxed the muscles of the mouth and neck, and yielded to the bit to break him of the habits of bolting, shying, kicking and running away.

You must require this of every part of his body, and watch for it in every step of your training. And never forget to caress and encouraging him for re laxing the muscles and giving up.

To Catch and Halter the Colt.

Walk round the colt as gently as possible in the pasture, working him in quietly towards the barn yard or an enclosure, then open the barn doors and hitch an old horse on the back part of the barn floor, then commence walking round and about the colt, and whistle and sing, and gradually approach the colt on the side opposite the barn, keeping your back towards him.

Do not face the colt and undertake to crowd him into the barn, for by so doing you will attract the attention of the colt, and he will be likely to become suspicious of danger, and attempt to escape. In a few moments the colt will walk into the barn, close the doors and get out the old horse as best you can, getting alone with the colt. Never attempt to

educate the colt or break the horse of any bad habit
in the open street, where other objects can attract
his attention ; for while one thing is occupying the
horse's mind, it is hard to teach him what you want
him to do, or make an impression that will be last-
ing. Now let the colt examine you for a few moments. If you can approach then and lay your hand
on him cautiously, you will soon gain his confidence, and thereby rid him of all fear of you. But
if he is very wild, turns his heels towards you, stands
and trembles, and attempts to kick whenever you
approach him, prepare yourself with a pole, not less
than ten or twelve feet in length, drive two nails, one
about an inch from the end, and the other about
twelve inches from it, and parallel with it, sticking
about an inch out of the pole. Take the headstall
part of your halter, or that which lies back of the
ears, and hang it upon the two nails at the side of
the pole, so that in twisting the pole it will fall off,
make the noose of your common rope halter large by
pulling the stale through the loop, so that it will
pass over the head readily. Now grasp the pole at
the opposite end and approach your colt. The moment he sees it, it will attract his attention and he
will turn towards it to examine it, while he is smel-
ling of it you pass it quietly back of the ears, then
turn the nails down, and the halter will drop upon
his neck. Now with the end of the pole push up
the loop and draw up the stale and your colt is hal-
tered.

To Handle the Colt·

Next with the smooth end of the pole tickle the colt about the neck, when he feels this, it answers the place of a caress, and will quiet him, then gradually approach your colt shortening your hold of the pole and taking in your halter stale at the same time, when you get within arms length use your hand in the same place ; keep on handling and caressing your colt about the head and ears.

If the colt holds his head high and will not let you put on the war bridle, put your hand over the back of the head or neck and bear with a steady presure until he relaxes the muscles and ducks his head. When he does this encourage him by caressing. Repeat the same operation until he will put his head in any position that you desire.

Then commence handling the colt, commencing at the sholder and rubbing every part of the leg clear to the hoof, till he stands quietly. Now put one hand against the shoulder and crowd against the colt throwing the weight upon the opposite foot, with the other hand at the fetlock, raise the foot from the ground only a little ways, and put it right down again, do not carry it high enough or hold it long enough to frighten the colt so that he will make an effort to jerk it away from you ; for if he does he will repeat it every time you take it from the ground, after caressing the leg a little while lift it a little higher and put it right down as at first. Repeat this process until he relaxes the muscles and will allow you to hold the foot as long as you like.

Take next a hammer and tap on it as if shoeing it, rasping and tapping it in every position required by the blacksmith. Now gradually work along his body to the hind foot, by carressing him, which you will handle in the same way, never attempting to grapple with the muscle of a strong horse, but teach them by kindness to relax the muscles of the leg which is an infallible sign that they are willing you should handle the foot as you please.

Handle the feet on the other side in the same way, as handling on one side will not answer for the other. Next commence handling the Colt's tail, lifting it by steady pressure, till the muscles relax. When the muscles do relax give him his tail and caress him. Repeat the operation till you get perfect control of the tail, caressing as he yields. Having thus rid your colt of all fear of yourself, he is prepared to be taught to lead in halter.

To Teach the Colt to Lead.

Put on the " War Bridle." Never at first attempt to pull your Colt ahead, for his strength is greater than yours, if he resists ; but place yourself in such a position that you can force him to move in the direction required. Take your position over the point of the hip, give the word of command, " come here, sir," in a loud and distinct tone of voice, at the same time give a sudden jerk on the cord which will compell him to move towards you, say " whoa" and caress him, to assure him that he has done all that you require of him. Step round to the other side and repeat the movements, keeping your eye on the colt's eye. Whenever you see his eye be-

ginning to follow you as you walk round to get
your position, say "come here, sir," without jerk-
ing him and he will turn towards you. Accept
of anything towards what you want, and caress
him for it.

Repeat the operation until he will follow you
round and round on either side. If at any time he
neglects to answer the word of command, punish
him by a sudden yank on the cord. Now step out
in front, give the word of command and a light
yank and learn him to come in that direction. In
a very short time you will teach him to follow you
anywhere by the word of command.

To Teach the Colt to follow under Crack of the Whip.

Hold the "War Bridle" in one hand, and with
the other crack the whip over and about him. At
first he is frightened at the sound, but the "War
Bridle" brings him to you when you cease cracking
the whip. Reward him for coming by caressing.
He soon learns to come to you for protection.

To Bit the Colt.

It will facilitate the bitting of the Colt to lay him
down a few times, which will make him yield his
mouth and give in to the bit more readily, then put
the "War Bridle" about the neck, making the loop

large, so as to slip down over the withers or sit snugly where the collar rests, to get the leverage to draw in the neck, then bring the loop through and put it in his mouth. Now stand in front of your Colt and draw steadily upon the cord, and wait for a sign; when he relaxes the muscle of his mouth and neck and 'ducks' his head, ease up on the cord and caress him, which says to the horse, "that is right. Whenever you feel restraint in the mouth with the bit curb your head, and get up in style." If you wish to get the head higher after curbing it, give an upward throw of the cord and he will raise the head, for which caress him.

Repeat the operation till the Colt thoroughly understands, and yields to the bit, which is all you can do by any process of bitting.

To Train to Harness.

Always break your colt in single harness; for when properly broken single there is no trouble in driving double. Use the "War Bridle" till you have finished harnessing him. To repress any uneasiness or fear of the harness, take the harness in one hand and approach the Colt's head, letting him examine it, passing it over his head and about his body to rid him of fear. If he attempts to move out of the way, punish him with a yank on the "War Bridle;" when again quiet, caress him, and proceed with the harnessing. Put the lines through the fill-straps instead of through the turrets, which will allow them to drop down about the hams.

This will give you control of the horse's body, so that you can force it to move at the word of command.

The first thing to teach the colt, is to move ahead at the word of command, which you may do by giving the word of command, and at the same time tapping him lightly with the whip, but not hard enough to hurt him. As soon as he moves, however slightly, say "whoa," and caress him, and assure him by caressing that his motion was right. Repeat till he moves readily at the word of command.

Now you want him to obey the side rein, and turn to right or left promptly. Your horse is in harness, not hitched to any vehicle. Now with reins in hand, step six or eight feet behind the horse, and as many feet to the right. Now pulling the rein in the left hand, you will throw the hinder part off its balance and towards you drawing the head to the left, which causes him to wheel about in the direction required. When the horse moves, say "whoa," and caress him. Then step as far to the left side and in the rear, and pull on the lines in your right hand, which will force him to turn to the right; and when he moves, say "whoa," and caress him. Repeat these operations until he relaxes the muscles of the neck and mouth, and yields willingly to the side rein. By this process of forcing the body to move, the Colt soon gets the idea that resistance is useless, and he will turn so far as the reins direct and no farther.

To Teach the Colt to Back.

Use the reins through the fill-straps the same as above. All that is necessary to teach the colt to back, is to get the first move in the right direction, and then stop him and caress, assuring him that that is right, which you do as follows :—

Step about four paces back and two to the right, now say distinctly, " back," and at the same time give a sudden pull upon both reins. The left rein drawing about his hips, will throw him off his balance and force him to move his feet from the ground. The right rein prevents his turning, and gives a backward move. When he moves, if he takes but one step, say "whoa," and caress him. Step to the other side and repeat the operation in that direction, encouraging as before, but never caress until the horse stands perfectly still, for running back is as bad a habit as not to back at all. To give the horse a chance to understand the word of command, start him ahead and stop him with the word of command and start him a little way back and stop him with the word of command, repeating this operation for some time, caressing as he obeys your directions.

To Drive in Shafts.

Here is where many fail in breaking Colts, by supposing that because the Colt drives well double that he should also know all about driving in shafts, which is a great mistake, for he either imagines himself so confined that he cannot move his feet, or is confused by the action of the reins in the mouth, or is frightened with the shafts at his heels and begins kicking. There is no place that we can put a Colt that requires such careful management and patient teaching as when we put him first in shafts. I regard mismanagement in this step of his training, as the cause of making more balky, kiching, and runaway horses than all others put together, which habits may be more easily avoided than cured, by proceeding as follows :—

Prepare yourself with a cart—an axletree and a pair of shafts, having a good strong cross-bar, is all that is required. So arrange your shafts that the cross-bar will be sufficiently high to strike the horse about half way between the hock and haunch bone. Now back your cart against a post, bring your colt round and let him look at it and examine it, then turn your colt's heels near the ends of the shafts, raise the shafts and draw a little ahead, then commence gently rubbing it up and down the hind leg to rid him of fear concerning it, then draw the cart ahead and put the shafts through the fill straps, hook up the tugs, but do not put on any hold-back straps; I never use any hold-backs on any horse until he is thoroughly broken and rid of all fear of his heels. You have taught your colt to back, now let that be the first thing you ask him to do in shafts; step quietly behind your colt and say " back," and at the same time pull upon the reins, backing the cart against the post. When the cross-bar is about to strike his heels, give a sudden pull on the reins, so as to get the advantage of your colt by elevating his head. Hold him back firmly on the cross-bar until he ceases strugling, then ease up on the lines and

let him straighten up. Now shove the cart back-
wards and forwards against his heels, until he cares
nothing about it. Now when you turn your colt
to either side and his hind legs strike against the
shafts, he will not be frightened and commence
kicking. You have only to teach him that he can
turn in a pair of shafts, which you do by stepping
opposite the left shoulder, pulling the left rein entirely out of the turret, and give the word of command for your horse to start, and force him to turn
round shortly by pulling on this rein, stopping occa-
sionally to encourage by caressing. As the colt
begins to turn willingly, take your position more
and more behind, so as to get a direct draft on the
mouth, then step to the other side and force him to
turn to the right. Now step behind your colt and drive
for a little while with both reins swinging at the
side so as to get a greater side draft, to show your
colt what to do. Turning first to the right and then
to the left, till he turns readily to either side. Now,
put the reins in the turrets, and try to turn him on
short corners If he should at any time begin to
run back and appear to balk, do not begin to
whip, for he is only confused with the new action
in the mouth, which you give by putting the reins
through the turrets. Pull the rein out of the turret
and show him once more what to do, and you will
have a colt thoroughly broke, that you can depend
on at all times. The whole of this can be done in
about one hour's time.

How to Ride the Wild Colt.

Stand upon the near side of your colt and throw over his back a piece of web or strap, and fasten to his right forefoot below the fetlock joint ; then take up his foot and hold it for a few minutes until he ceases struggling, then quietly let him have it, and lead him along a few steps and say whoa, and at the same time you say whoa, draw up the strap, which makes him stop, for it puts him on three legs. After you have led him a little ways in this way, stand by his side and take up his foot and wind your hand in the strap, and commence to jump up and down by his side a few times, keeping hold of the foot, then carefully jump on him with your breast and slide back again, then while holding up his foot quietly jump on his back. Now let down his foot, and if he shows the least disposition to stir take up his foot and drop it, and take it again. The idea is, that he cannot think of two things at once, and the moment he thinks of throwing you off— (which you detect by the drawing of the muscles of his back,) you take up his foot and change his attention to that and his back is all right. This plan will ride any colt or horse.

To Prevent a Horse getting Cast in Stall.

Tie a ring on the halter, back of the ears, fasten another directly over his head in the stable, tie a cord into the one above and let it drop to within eighteen inches of the floor ; take this point and tie to the ring in the back of the head. No horse can roll without he can get the back of his head on the ground, to use as a lever to turn himself with.

Halter Pulling.

Prepare yourself with a good cord about the size of a bed-cord, about eighteen or twenty feet long, take the centre of the cord and put under the tail, where the crupper rests; cross them on the rump above the tail, to keep them in place, bring one strand on each side of the neck, and put through the rings of the halter, then hitch to the post or manger where you want your horse to pull.

You must now take some means to make your horse fly back suddenly. You will find the following a very good way:—Tie a piece of rotten cord in the halter, and hitch to the same post or manger, about eight or ten inches shorter than the one under the tail. He will break this rotten cord with a slight pull, which will give him a sudden lurch back on the cord under the tail; you then whip him over the head or frighten him with objects of fear, until he will not attempt to back. This will break up the worst puller in five minutes after the cord is adjusted.

Horse Bad to Shoe Behind.

Put on the "war bridle," and hold in the left hand, just over the loins, and just so as to straighten the cord to the colt's mouth. With the right hand commence to handle the colt's hind leg; if he should move it from the ground, reprove him with a jerk of the cord, and say "whoa." The force of this jerk will cause him to stop,

but do not begin to pat him to get him still, but say
" whoa," again, and give another jerk on the cord, and
repeat the punishment in the mouth until he gets still,
then pat him for doing what you asked, " whoa."

Now take a common pole-strap and rattle about his
leg until he is rid of fear ; then place the strap in front
of the posterior joint, just above the hoof, with the buckle
in the right hand, with one third of the strap on the side
the buckle is on, pass both ends of the strap behind the
foot and cross firmly under the fetlock, then bring both
ends in front of the shin bone and cross, then bring the
long end of the strap up over the ham-string above the
hock, and buckle on the outside, tight enough so the horse
cannot touch the foot to the ground.

When the foot is buckled up, if the horse does not try
to lean or kick, take hold of the halter and set him whirl-
ing round, and make him test it. If he should commence
leaning or kicking as soon as the strap is on, let him work
until the leg gets quiet. Now take hold of the foot and
see if he has relaxed the muscles, and will allow you
to handle it. If he should try to jerk, lean, or kick, do
not try to hold him, you are not strong enough—let go of
the leg, the strap will catch him. Take the foot in every
position the blacksmith will want it, being careful to
give it to him every time he attempts to take it away.
When he will allow you to handle it take a hammer and
tap on it as in the act of shoeing, until he cares nothing
about it ; then treat the other hind foot in the same way.
You need not be afraid of hurting the horse, as the strap
lies perfectly flat from beginning to end, and there is no

horse but that will give in to it in a few minutes, and allow you to shoe them.

The Horse Bad to Shoe Forward

Usually the horses bad to shoe forward are also bad to shoe behind ; so I would put on the strap as directed for the hind feet, and let him fight it out there, and they will usually show no resistance forward. But if they should, put on the "War Bridle," and say to the Blacksmith, "take up the foot and go to work, and if he moves a muscle, do not try to hold it, but let him take the foot," and at the same time you say "whoa," and punish him in the mouth with the cord until he stands still. Then take up the foot again, and go to work.

Jumping Fences.

Get six hame straps, four, inch-rings and two pieces of rope or cord. Take two of the hame straps and pass through a ring and buckle one of them around the hind leg, just above the hock, and the other just below the hock, just tight enough so as to keep them in place. Put two more on the other hind leg in the same way. Then put a ring on each of the other hame straps and buckle one on each fore leg, just below the knee—Now put a good leather circingle on your horse—Now take one cord and fasten in the ring on the hind leg, pass over the cir-

cingle and down to the ring on the fore leg, and tie. Put
the other cord on the other side in the same way. Now
you have your horse so fixed that he can walk about, lay
down, and get up, just as well as if there was nothing on
him, and he will not realize that there is anything to in-
terfere with his jumping, and when he makes the effort
he expects, in good faith to go over the fence ; but when
he rears up and throws out the fore feet to get over the
fence he jerks the hind ones out from under him, and he
falls back on the same side of the fence. He will repeat
this only a very few times before he will entirely give up
the habit, and you can take off the straps and let him
run.

Kicking in Stall.

Put on the rig the same as for fence jumping, with the
exception of buckling the straps on the fore legs below
the fetlock instead of above, now when he throws back
the hind foot to kick he jerks the fore foot from under
him. He will repeat until he expects to get caught in
the same trap every time and give up the habit.

Pawing in Stall.

For pawing in the stall put on the rig as for kicking in
stall. When he reaches out the fore foot to paw, it takes
the hind foot from under him, and he is cured.

To Trot Without Breaking.

Men often spend months and even years to teach a horse what might be taught with a judicious use of my plan in a very few days. And in fact at the end of long months of practice they have not accomplished what they desired; that their horse should stick to his work without breaking. In many cases the horse breaks worse than when they commenced. I claim, that with my plan you can so thoroughly control your horse and fix upon his mind the idea that he cannot break, that he can be depended upon at all times.

Now take four hame straps and two rings and buckle around the hind legs the same as for jumping fence. Then put on your standing martingals, on the lower end of which you put a good smooth ring. Now take a piece of good cord or pliable strap, and fasten into the ring on one hind foot, bring forward and pass through the ring on the standing martingals, then back to the ring on the other hind leg and tie; taking up all the slack cord. He has free use of his limbs to trot, as the cord renders through the ring on the martingal, and one foot pays out as fast as the other takes up, but when he breaks both feet go back at the same time which gives him a check in the mouth, and punishes him every step he takes.

Put your horse to trotting and when he breaks do not begin to say "whoa" and stop him with the lines as is the common practice, but put on the whip and say "go long" and keep on whipping and urging, and give no peace until he strikes a trot, then reach out over your sulky dash, and pat him, which says "you are now doing right." A horse may be made to be so afraid of the whip in this way that whenever it strikes him, it will be a warning not to break.

Hugging the Rein with the Tail.

Take the crupper and wind it with rags or something soft until you have a roll that is 3 or 4 inches in diameter, and then put it under his tail and let him hug it. He will have no power to hug the tail below this roll, and every time he throws it over the rein, as you rein your team, you pull it from under the tail in spite of him, which in a little while will rid him of all fear of his tail, and you can remove the roll.

The Switch-tail.

To cure the horse of switching his tail, use the roll under the tail the same as above which must be worn until the habit is entirely cured which in bad cases often takes three or four weeks; but it will affect a cure in time, and it is the only thing that will, that I know of.

Bad to Crupper,

Put on the "War Bridle," then step back close to the horse's hip and commence to handle the tail by lifting gently, but do not jerk, very soon the muscles will relax and give way, then give him his tail and caress. Repeat until he gives up willingly. If he should stir at any time, reprove him with the "War Bridle" and say 'whoa

Biting and Kicking when being Cleaned or Harnessed,

Put on the "War Bridle" and go to work. If he should kick or bite say "whoa," and reprove with a jerk of the "War Bridle," when he gets still go to work again. If he should be very vicious to bite, lay him down in the way described under the head of "To lay the horse down;"then use the "War Bridle" as above.

The Striking Horse.

Try to ascertain what is the cause of his striking, which you will generally find it to be that he dislikes to have you handle his nose. Put on the "War Bridle" and then touch him on the nose ; when he rears to strike, say "whoa," and give a sudden jerk of the cord, which will bring him down very quickly. Repeat this a few times and he will not dare to rear or strike.

Crowding or Kicking at you in Stall.

If a horse has the habit of leaning against you or of kicking at you when you pass into the stall, put on the war bridle and lead your horse into the stall, and hitch him, with the halter, keeping the war bridle in your hand as you pass out of the stall. Drive a nail or peg in the side of the stall to hang the cord on. You leave the horse for a little while, then attempt to pass in beside him, taking up the cord as you go out. When he attempts to come towards you, or kick at you, say "stand round, sir," and give a jerk on the cord, which will bring his head to you and throws his hind parts over in the stall. Then caress him, and repeat as often as necessary.

THE WAR BRIDLE.

This is one of the most powerful weapons I have in controling the horse. It is perfectly wounderful to see how quick you can thoroughly cure the horse of some bad habits by the use of this simple cord. If you put it on as here described, you will have nearly ten times as much power over the horse, as you would on the Rarey plan.

Get a cord 16 or 18 feet long, $\frac{3}{8}$ of an inch in diameter, of the best Russia hemp or sash cord, tie a knot on one end, just as you would to prevent its ravelling, now tie another knot about 20 inches from the one on the end, put this cord round the colts neck and pass the knot on the end through the other, any other knot that will not slip up and choke the colt will do as well. Now pass your hand under this cord in the direction from head to to shoulder and draw the cord through double to make a loop which you put in the horse's mouth.

To Lay the Horse Down.

There is nothing, probably, that we can do with the horse, that will satisfy him in so short a space of time that we can handle him as we like, and will give us such thorough control of the horse as laying him down a few times; especially if done in the way I am about to describe. Yet, all the plans hitherto brought forward have been objectionable, on account of the great liability of injuring the horse, and also of getting injured yourself, which is entirely done away with, in my plan, and not only this, but it helps you to get control of the mouth faster than you can in any other way.

Get a good strong leather circingle and put it on your horse. Then take the crupper strap out of your harness and tie it to the circingle on the back, and put the crupper under the tail. Now take a cord or strap, and fasten to the crupper strap on the rump, then fasten to the circingle on the off side of the horse, about half way from the back to the belly, to act as a brace to the circingle. Now tie a ring firmly to the circingle, right by the brace. Now take a good strong cord, 18 feet long, tie one end in

a hard knot around the neck, then pass through t
mouth from the near side, and then back through the ri
on off side of circingle. Now take a strap 18 inches lo;
and put it round the fetlock on the near fore foot. Th
take up the foot and buckle to the circingle. Now pr
on the cord from any direction, and you will turn tl
horse's head round to the right side, which will throw tl
heft of his body on the near side, where the foot is stra;
ped up, and he will have nothing to support him unt
his knee strikes the ground. He is then off his balanç
and must come down.

If he should rear from the ground, when he come
down he will not strike upon his knees as in other plans
and injure them, but will strike upon his off foot, thei
settle down on his knee again.

The beauties of this system are, that you save your horse
from all injury, and can stand far enough from your horse
to be perfectly safe yourself, and can lay him down much
easier and quicker: ten times in a minute if he can get
up quick enough, and at the same time control the horse's
mouth.

Kicking in Harness.

The horse that kicks in harness does it through fear, or
self-defence. He imagines, that as he has once got at
liberty by kicking the wagon or cutter to pieces, it is the
only way to get out of a dangerous position.

You should bare constantly in mind that there is no kicking, runaway, shying or bolting horse but that has a mouth that is perfectly uncontroled whenever he attempts to do either of the above habits.

With the kicking horse you must not only control his mouth, but rid him of all fear of his heels, whatever may be the cause of his kicking. There is no way that you can get control of his mouth so fast, as by laying him down. Which you should repeat until he quits fighting the cord, and lies down quietly.

Then put on the war bridle, and handle him to the right and left the same as for leading a colt, to get his attention, which will also help to control his mouth. Now get a double jointed bit made as follows : length, 8 inches from ring to ring ; the long bars to be 5½ inches and the short ones 2½ inches. When this is put into the mouth it shuts thus,

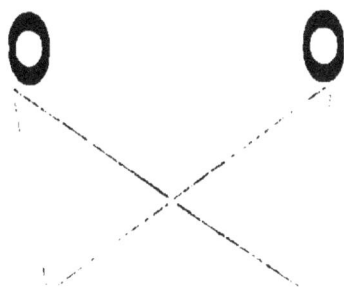

Put the horse to trotting round, say "whoa," and at the same time give a sudden roll of the bit, by pulling first one rein, then the other in quick succession. This

motion of the bit will not cut the mouth but will open it
and give him a sudden "whoa," for which you caress him,
but not til he is perfectly still. If he should keep stepping or backing say whoa, and repeat the roll of the bit,
until he is still then caress. Then start again and repeat
t ic "whoa" until he obeys quickly when spoken to.

Then take a cart with a strong crossbar, which should
be just high enough to strike him about half way between
the hock and the haunch bone. Hitch your horse to the
cart without holdback straps, and back him against the
post. As the crossbar is about to strike him, you get
advantage of your horse by giving a sudden roll of the
bit, which will get his head up and set him over on the
crossbar, where you hold him firmly until he ceases struggling, then let him straighten up and commence to shove
the cart backward and forward on his heels until he
cares nothing about it, then rattle things about his heels
to rid of fear, then start him trotting round, say "whoa,
and give a roll of the bit, and make him stop the cart
with his heels, hold it firmly against him and make him
back it.

Repeat this until you are satisfied he will not kick any
more.

The Kicking Horse on account of Line under the Tail.

Control the mouth as above. Then put in the cart and back against the post, hold there and put one line under the tail, which you rattle about until he relaxes the tail and lets it up. Then pull from under the tail, as you would in reining your team, then repeat until he will not hug the line.

The Horse that Kicks when touched with the Whip.

Back against the post as above, and tap him all over with the whip until he cares nothing about it.

To Rid the Horse of Fear of Whip. Umberella Buffalo and other Objects.

Back against the post as above, then commence moving the whip through the air, then crack but do not hit him. When he finds he cannot get away from it, and it does not hurt him, he will give up. You must repeat until he will not flinch a muscle.

With the robe and umberella, hold him back against the post and let some person approach him with them, and carry all around him until he cares nothing about them.

Runaway Horse·

Handle precisely the same as for kicking in harness. No horse will attempt to run away after you get thorough control of the mouth.

Bolting Horse·

Give him a good "whoa" the same as for kicking in harness. Then with the reins through the fill straps, set him travelling round until he bolts. Then take this occasion to give him a good exercise on a side rein, swinging the body to the right and left, as fast as you can, until he relaxes the muscles of the mouth and neck ; which you can tell by the feeling of the reins. When you have perfect obedience on a side rein he will not bolt any more.

Shying Horse·

The shying horse I regard simply as a bolting horse, neither will obey a side rein. The only difference that exists between them is, that the shyer bolts when he is frightened, while the bolter bolts when he sees a favorable opportunity to go in to a yard or barn. Never strike the horse with the whip for shying, for he is in a state of excitement and will think it is the object he sees that hurts him, or expects to get whipped whenever he is frightened, and will bolt into the ditch and run away ;

but thoroughly control the mouth, the same as for bolting, so that he neither dare turn to the right or left, but stands perfectly still, and examines the object for a moment. Then approaches and passes by without doing you any harm. If you give him time to examine it, he will not be afraid of it again.

Balky Horse.

There are several kinds of balky horses, and I treat each kind differently. Try to assertain how your horse acts, when he baulks, or what is the cause of his baulking, and then go to work to remove the cause. Some horses are very sensitive and require nice handling. You should use a great deal of coolness and judgment in the treatment of these horses We will take first what I call.

Mouth Balker.

This horse is restless and uneasy and will not stand until told to go. He leaps and jumps or runs when he starts. If allowed to go, when he gets ready, he may quiet down after driving a short distance, and drive all day without any more trouble; but if held by the reins until he is told to go, he will balk and refuse to stir. This horse only needs controling in the mouth, and educating on the bit.

First lay him down a few times. It will help to get control of the mouth. Then handle with the war bridle, to get his attention, then put on the bit, and give him a "whoa," then put in the cart and back against the post. as for "kicking in harness," then tell him to go, when he will begin to prance and lunge. as usual. When he makes the lunge set him back, with a roll of the bit: which you repeat until he is quiet, then tell him to go again, and when he makes another lunge, set him back again, and repeat until he steps forward on the walk a few steps. When he does start on the walk say "whoa" and caress. Be careful that you do not let him walk until he begins to prance again; for then you would loose the opportunity of teaching him the idea, that walking is what you want. Now let him do nothing but walk, until he is thoroughly satisfied and willing to walk and obey the bit. Get out and in the wagon often, as if you were going to start, but do not let him go until told, nor do not tell him to go as long as there is a muscle in motion; for so long as he paws the ground, or shakes his head, it is as bad, as if he were prancing or jumping. He should have two lessons the one just described should be in some quiet place, where you can have his whole attention. The next in the streets. Now you have only to call his attention to the bit, and make him walk for an hour or two all over town. You will be very much surprised at the wonderful change that has come over your horse, while trotting, he was all excitement and ambitious to go faster, but while walking is cool, and sees his mistake.

The Horse that will not stand for you to get into the Wagon.

Many horses that are not balky, will not stand until told to go. Handle them precisely the same as the mouth balker, if bad, if not bad give them a good "whoa" with the bit, and get out and in until they are satisfied, and never let them go until they are quiet.

The Sulky Balker.

This horse stands perfectly still, and would submit to be whipped nearly to death, before he would stir, more than to turn and look at you.

One Way.—He will neither go for the whip nor any ordinary word of command, so teach him a new one. After laying down, &c, put him in the cart without any load. Stand on the near side and by his fore foot. Rest your right hand on his withers to balance you, with the left hand take hold of the reins, and draw his head towards you This will incline him to move a little. Then give the word, and at the same time touch him with your foot sharply on the big tendon, just below the knee, this will make him take the foot up and start ahead before he thinks of the cart, say "whoa" before he stops, and caress for drawing the cart. Repeat until he goes readily every time spoken to, and as far as you like, which you have taught him by gradually increasing the distance.

Now you wish him to draw a load, which you teach him by putting on a little at first, and repeating the word, then a little more and so on until he draws all you wish him to draw.

Now you wish to get into the wagon and ride. Take the reins in the left hand, and your whip stalk in the right. Step back a little and touch the foot with the whip stalk, to call his attention there. Repeat a few times, and step back a little farther, and so on, until you get into the wagon. Then you crack your whip lash round the fore foot and give the word, and away he goes.

You have given the horse no chance to get out of temper for he has gone before he thought of the load. You have stopped him before he was discouraged, and encouraged him by caressing until he is perfectly satisfied to go when spoken to.

ANOTHER WAY.—We may often get caught with a baulky horse with a load on. When we have not the time to go through with the system of education described above, and would be glad to know how to start him and go on with the load.

Take a cord or strap and tie around one of the fore legs, just below the knee, then step directly in front of your horse, and take the foot from under him by pulling on the cord. He will struggle to take the foot from you, but hold it firmly drawing as far a head as possible. Watch his moves, for he will very soon try to get the oot to the ground by going ahead. When he makes the forward move, give him the foot, and at the same time tell him to go, and he must draw the load.

Now all depends upon your encouraging the horse at the right time, so do not let him go until he is out of temper or stops of his own accord; but after he has gone a few steps say "whoa," and caress. Then repeat as before, and he will, generally in a short time, go at the word of command.

To Make a True Horse Break a Balky One,

ONE WAY.—No matter whether the horse pulls at the halter or not, put the cord under the tail and hitch to a post the same as for pulling at halter. Hit him over the head with the whip and he will fly back against the cord. Just as the cord strikes the tail you say "go-long" and he moves ahead, for which you caress. When he will not touch the cord any more, hitch him up in harness with the true horse. Leave the cord under the tail, and pass through his inside turret ring. Now take a good stiff poll that is long enough to reach from one foot back of the double whiffletree to the horses nose. Now fasten one end of the poll to the inside end of the true horses single whiffletree, letting it run back over the double tree 12 or 14 inches to prevent getting tangled. Now pass a strap or piece of webbing, from the hame-ring of one horse to the hame-ring of the other, as a support to the poll. Tie the ends of the cord to the upper end of the poll. Take hold of the reins and tell your team to go. When the true horse starts ahead of the balking one he shoves the poll ahead and tightens the cord under the balky ones tail which will bring him up. Stop and caress every time he moves. Repeat until he will go at the word of command.

ANOTHER WAY.—Handle with the war bridle until he will spring ahead with the least pull. Adjust the poll as described above, and fasten the war bridle to the upper end of the poll in place of the cord under the tail. Give a few inches slack to the war bridle, so as not to touch him when he goes all right.

You will now have the whole strength of the true horse to shove him out on the war bridle and he must go.

The Backing Balker.

Hitch to the cart without buckeling the hold-back straps. Tell him to go ahead, and when he begins to back, guide the cart to the post and back his heels violently against the crossbar a few times, until he is sick of backing, and shows a willingness to go ahead. Then tell him to go, and if he starts off say "whoa" and caress.

If this does not answer, put the cord under his tail the same as for pulling at halter. Straighten him up in the shafts, and hitch one end of the cord to the end of one shaft and the other end to the other shaft. Now when he backs, there being no hold-backs on, it catches him under the tail and he must stop backing and go ahead. Then stop and caress. Repeat again till he draws freely at the word of command.

The Balker that throws Himself in Harness.

As I have said, in another place, we should always place ourselves in a position to command the horse's body, and never ask him to do anything until we are prepared to move the body where we wish it to go; but with this horse, we can take no position in which we can force him to come to his feet and stand there. But we can teach him to do so and at the same time teach him to draw at the word of command. I teach him to draw not in laying him down, but in getting him up. I have never seen one of this class of horses but that, after throwing a few times, would balk on the ground and refuse to get up.

Do not care s for coming down as you would another horse; but throw him down roughly until he refuses to get up. Then give the same word of command in a sharp quick tone, that you would give to have him draw "get up or go long, and at the same time stike him spightfully with a raw-hide or whip across the muscles of the nose; for there is no other place on his body, where so little whipping will bring him to his feet as here. Caress him for getting up and standing there. Throw him again and repeat until he will spring to his feet whenever he hears the word that you have used.

Hitch him to a load, and he will draw every time he hears the same word.

TRICKS !

As many may wish to know how to teach their horses tricks I will explain how it may be done. Teaching a young horse a few tricks serves greatly to keep up an interest in him and makes him appear intelligent, fearless and affectionate. In teaching your horse to perform tricks it is best to give him one or two lessons, of half or three-quarters of an hour each, daily.

To Come at the Crack of the Whip or at the Word of Command,

Put on the war bridle, stand off a few feet from his head holding the end of the bridle in your left hand and the whip in the right; crack the whip a little and say come here sir; he does not know what this means but you show him by pulling on the bridle a little which he will obey by moving towards you a few steps; for this movement you thank him by stepping foiward and giving him a little apple, or a few kernels of corn, and caressing him gently ; then repeat in the same way, rewarding him as before, and so continue until he will walk up to you readily when you crack the whip or say come here sir, which he will soon learn to do. Each time he comes to you talk to him kindly and do not fail to give him his little reward of corn, apple, oats, or something of the kind which he likes. You a now take off his halter and turn him loose and re at until he fully comprehends that the way to avoid the whip is to come to you, which, with the encouragement of rewarding him, will soon inspire his fullest confidence, and he will come to you and follow like a dog. Be very cautious about the use of the whip or harsh language, remembering that perfect, cheerful obedience is your object and that can be secured only by great patience and gentleness.

TO MAKE A BOW.

Take a pin in your right hand between the thumb and fore-finger, and stand up before but a little to the left of your horse, then prick him on the breast very lightly as if a fly biting, which to relieve he will bring down his head, which you will accept as yes, and for which you will reward him by caressing and feeding as before, then repeat and so continue until he will bring his head down the moment he sees the least motion of your hand towards his breast, or substitute some signal which he will understand readily.

TO SAY "NO."

Stand by your horse near the shoulder holding the same pin in your hand, with which prick him lightly on the withers : to drive which away he will shake his head, you then caress as before, and repeating until he will shake his head at the least indication of your touching him with the pin. You can train your horse so nicely in this way in a short time as to cause him to shake his head or bow by merely turning the hand a little, or moving it slightly towards him.

TO LIE DOWN.

To teach a horse to do this quickly, lay him down repeatedly, as described in another place When he begins to come down without resistance, give the word of command "Lie Down Sir". Then caress to encourage him for coming down. When he does this readily, let down the foot that has been strapped up. Then, if it is the near fore foot that has been strapped up, grasp that about the fetlock with the left hand, and take hold of the cord with the right hand over the horses back, say " lie down sir" and pull on the end keeping hold of the foot and drawing it well back. Repeat until he comes down readily this way. Then take a switch and touch his foot, which will cause him to take it from the ground, and pull on the cord, and he will lie down. Gradually slacken the cord until he will come down by touching his foot. Repeat this until he will come down whenever told.

TO SIT UP.

When your horse will lie down readily you can teach him to sit up like a dog easily. If young and not very heavy and strong you can easily prevent his getting up without tying down. First cause him to lie down, having on him a common bridle with the reins over the neck, then step behind him and place the right foot firmly upon the tail, the reins in your hands, then say get up sir. The horse rising from a recumbent position, first turns on his belly, throws out his forward feet and raises himself on them, springs forward, and rises on his hind feet. Now standing upon his tail firmly and pulling back upon the reins when he attempts to spring forward and up will prevent his doing so, and you hold him sitting up.—Hold him firmly a few seconds. talking to him kindly, before permitting him to rise on his feet. Repeat a few times when, instead of springing up he will sit on his haunches a short time which you are to accept as complying with your wishes. Always say sit up sir every time, and hold him in his position as long as he will bear by fondling and feeding him with something he likes from the hand, and your horse will soon learn to sit up for you as long as you please. But if your horse is heavy and strong it will be necessary to resort to other means to hold him down at first. This you do by putting on his back a common collar and causing him to lie down. Then fasten a piece of rope or a rein to each hind foot and bring forward through the collar and draw up close, which will bring the hind feet well forward. Then step behind as before and when he attempts to rise on his hind feet he finds it impossible to do so because you hold them firmly with those straps. Repeat two or three times when it will not be necessary to resort to such force.

To Teach Your Horse To Kiss You·

Teach him first to take an apple out of your hand. Then gradually raise the hand nearer your mouth at each reception until you require him to take it from your mouth, holding it with the hand, telling him at the same time to kiss you. He will soon learn to reach his nose up to your mouth, first to get the apple, but finally because commanded to do so. Simply repeat until your horse understands the trick thoroughly.

TO SHAKE HANDS.

Tie a short strap or a piece of cord to the forward foot below the fetlock. Stand directly before the horse, hold the end of this strap or cord in your hand, then say, shake hands sir ; and immediately after commanding him to do so pull upon the strap, which will bring his foot forward and which you are to accept as shaking hands, thanking him for it by caressing and feeding, and so repeat until when you make the demand he will bring the foot forward in anticipation of having it pulled up. This is a very easy trick to teach a horse. By a little patience a horse may be easily trained to approach make a bow, shake hands and follow like a dog, lie

down, sit up, &c., which makes him appear both
polite and intelligent. Never lose courage or confidence in your ability because you may not bring
about good results easily. To accomplish anything of importance remember requires no ordinary
resolution or perseverance. There would be no
credit or importance attached to mastering and
managing bad horses if not difficult and apparently
dangerous. No duty requires more firmness of
purpose in the control of the passions, or more fi-
delity of the principles of kindness and truth, than
that of horsemanship. If you would be a really
successful horseman you must never seem to forget
by your conduct that you are a man, and that your
real superiority over the animal consists of the pru-
dent exercise of your reasoning powers. Brute
force is not your forte, and the instant you give way
to passion your reason must yield to the control of
blind instinct, and you at once abdicate your intel-
lectual superiority over the animal. Try to prove
by the example of your actions in the performance
of the duty that to be a good horseman requires
higher qualifications of fitness than that of huckster-
ing dishonesty and depravity so generally evinced
in the conduct of those claiming the distinction.

CONTENTS.

48

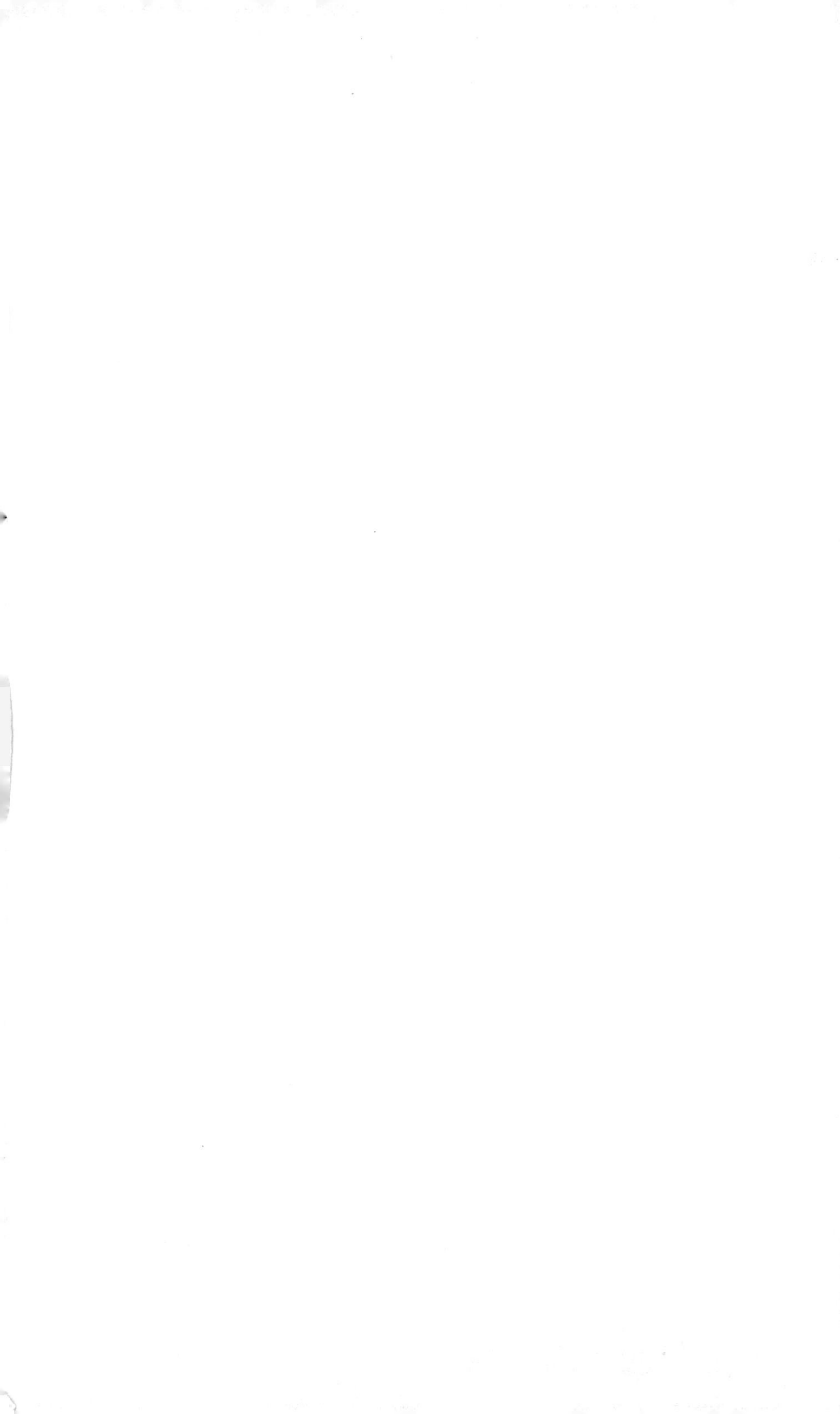